Fun Valentine's Day Crafts

Arlene and Herbert Erlbach

Enslow Elementary

an imprint of

Enslow Publishers, Inc.

40 Industrial Road
Box 398
Berkeley Heights, NJ 07922
USA

www.enslow.com

To Cely Weinstein, a person with a big heart.

Enslow Elementary, an imprint of Enslow Publishers, Inc.
Enslow Elementary® is a registered trademark of Enslow Publishers, Inc.

Copyright © 2015 by Enslow Publishers, Inc.

Originally published as *Valentine's Day Crafts* in 2004.

Library of Congress Cataloging-in-Publication Data

Erlbach, Arlene.
    [Valentine's Day crafts]
    Fun Valentine's Day crafts / Arlene and Herbert Erlbach.
        pages cm. — (Kid fun holiday crafts!)
    Audience: Grades K to grade 3.
    Includes bibliographical references and index.
    ISBN 978-0-7660-6255-9 — ISBN 978-0-7660-6257-3 (EPUB) — ISBN 978-0-7660-6258-0 (single-user PDF) —
        ISBN 978-0-7660-6259-7 (multi-user PDF) 1. Valentine decorations— Juvenile literature. 2. Valentines— Juvenile
        literature. I. Erlbach, Herb. II. Title.
    TT900.V34E75 2015
    745.594'1618— dc23
                    2014025019

Future editions:
Paperback ISBN: 978-0-7660-6256-6   EPUB ISBN: 978-0-7660-6257-3
Single-User PDF ISBN: 978-0-7660-6258-0   Multi-User PDF ISBN: 978-0-7660-6259-7

Printed in the United States of America

102014 Bang Printing, Brainerd, Minn.

10 9 8 7 6 5 4 3 2 1

To Our Readers: We have done our best to make sure all Internet addresses in this book were active and appropriate when we went to press. However, the author and the publisher have no control over and assume no liability for the material available on those Internet sites or on other Web sites they may link to. Any comments or suggestions can be sent by e-mail to comments@enslow.com or to the address on the back cover.

♻ Enslow Publishers, Inc., is committed to printing our books on recycled paper. The paper in every book contains 10% to 30% post-consumer waste (PCW). The cover board on the outside of each book contains 100% PCW. Our goal is to do our part to help young people and the environment too!

Illustration Credits: Crafts prepared by June Ponte; craft photography by Carl Feryok.

Cover Illustration: Craft prepared by June Ponte; craft photography by Kristin McCarthy and Carl Feryok.

CONTENTS

Introduction 4

1. Bag of Valentine Wishes 6

2. Friendship Necklace 8

3. Fold-up Valentine Surprise 10

4. Amore Napkin Rings........................... 12

5. Valentine Cat................................ 14

6. Lacy Valentine Bookmark..................... 16

7. Love Bug Card 18

8. Heart Ornament 20

9. Valentine Butterfly Paper Clip 22

10. Sun Catcher Heart............................ 24

    Patterns 26
    Read About Valentine's Day................... 29
    Index.. 31

Safety Note: Be sure to ask for help from an adult, if
needed, to complete these crafts!

INTRODUCTION

Each year we celebrate Valentine's Day on February 14. We send and receive heart-shaped cards. We eat red or pink candies and cookies. We tell our friends and family how much we care about them. No one is sure exactly how Valentine's Day began. It may have started 2,000 years ago. On a Roman holiday called Lupercalia, girls wrote their names on sheets of paper. They put them in a jug. A boy would pick a girl's name out of the jug. The two would become partners for the holiday. Sometimes, the couple would get engaged at the end of the celebration.

There is another story about a cruel Roman emperor who lived in the year 269. He did not want young men to marry. He wanted them for his army instead. A priest named Valentine secretly married the young couples. The emperor found out. On February 14, he had the priest killed.

A different story about Valentine's Day is about another priest who was also named Valentine. He was sent to prison because he refused to pray to the Roman gods. Valentine became friendly with a prison guard. The guard's blind daughter and Valentine fell in love.

Before the emperor had him killed, Valentine wrote the girl a letter. When she opened it, a miracle happened. She could see. The letter was signed "from your Valentine."

BAG OF VALENTINE WISHES

Make a collection of valentine wishes. Put them in a pretty bag to give as a present.

WHAT YOU WILL NEED

- small paper bag (about 4 x 6 inches)
- markers, glitter pens, crayons, or stickers
- construction paper
- scissors
- craft sticks
- white glue
- red or white tissue paper

WHAT TO DO

1. Decorate the paper bag with markers, glitter pens, crayons, or stickers.

2. Fold the sheet of red construction paper into rectangles.

3. Cut out the rectangles. Then, cut them into hearts. If you like, use the patterns on page 26.

4. Write messages on the back of the craft sticks.

5. Glue the paper hearts to the front of the craft sticks. Decorate the front of the sticks.

6. Place the tissue paper in your bag so that the valentine sticks can stand up. Arrange the valentine sticks in the bag.

Fold and cut your paper. Then, cut out hearts . . .

Start by decorating a bag . . .

Add colorful messages . . .

Share your great-looking bag with others!

Use the bag as a centerpiece for a Valentine's Day party. Or, give it to a special friend or relative as a holiday present.

FRIENDSHIP NECKLACE

This necklace is made by pasting materials made of paper to a surface. Then, they are sealed to make them permanent. This art form is called *decoupage*.

WHAT YOU WILL NEED

* poster board
* pencil
* scissors
* hole punch
* paper materials (gift wrap, construction paper, etc.)

* white glue
* small bowl or paper cup
* water
* paintbrush
* wax paper
* yarn

WHAT TO DO

1. Draw a heart shape on the poster board. If you like, use the pattern on page 26. Cut the heart out.

2. Glue on scraps of paper materials to decorate your heart. Let them dry on a sheet of wax paper.

3. In the small bowl or paper cup, mix up a thin glue "soup." Use three parts glue to one part water. Brush the glue mixture over the heart and let it dry overnight on the wax paper.

4. Cut your heart in half, puzzle style. Punch a hole at the top of each curve of the heart, as shown. Then, tie a piece of yarn through the hole in each half of the heart.

Make a puzzle-shaped cut . . .

Cut out a heart and add
colorful paper . . .

Share your finished necklace
with a friend!

HOLIDAY HINT:

Give one half of the necklace to a special friend.
Keep the other half to remind you of how important
you are to each other.

FOLD-UP VALENTINE SURPRISE

Inside this valentine there is a message and a surprise gift!

WHAT YOU WILL NEED

* red construction paper
* pencil
* scissors
* white glue
* doily
* stickers
* small toy or candy
* clear tape

WHAT TO DO

1. Fold both sheets of paper in half. Draw half a heart (use the pattern on page 26, if you like) on the fold of one of the pieces. Holding both sheets together, cut out the heart. This will give you two hearts of the same size.

2. Glue the hearts so that the bottom point of one heart is attached to the center of the other heart. Let the glue dry.

3. Write a message on the doily. Then, glue the doily to the center of the heart.

4. Decorate the hearts with stickers or paint markers. Tape a small toy or candy to the middle of the doily.

5. Fold the hearts to the center, as shown. Close the valentine with clear tape.

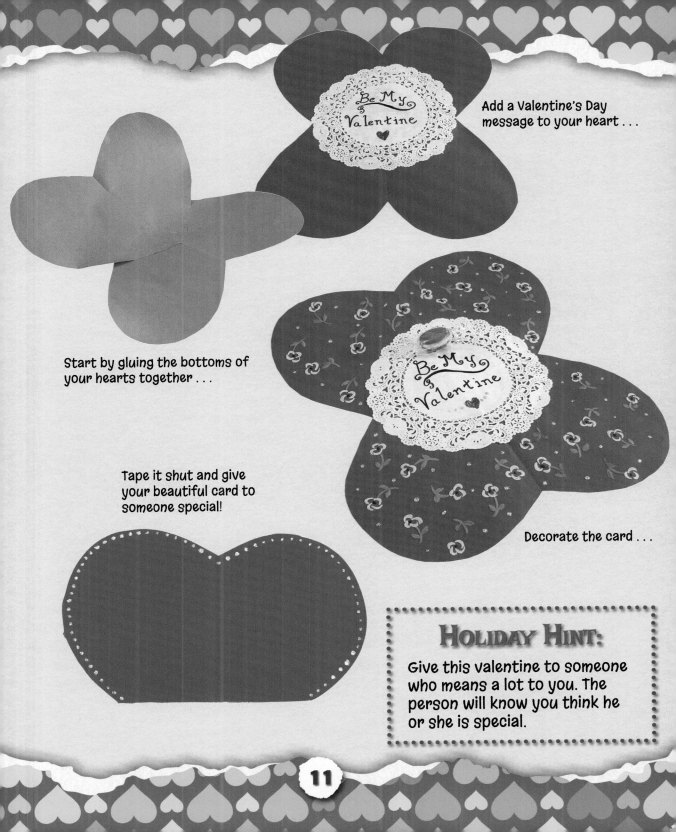

Add a Valentine's Day message to your heart . . .

Start by gluing the bottoms of your hearts together . . .

Be My Valentine

Tape it shut and give your beautiful card to someone special!

Be My Valentine

Decorate the card . . .

HOLIDAY HINT:

Give this valentine to someone who means a lot to you. The person will know you think he or she is special.

Amore Napkin Rings

Amore is Italian for "love." Set a pretty Valentine's Day table with these festive napkin rings.

What You Will Need

* empty toilet paper roll
* ruler
* pencil
* scissors

* red felt and felt in a contrasting color
* white glue

What To Do

1. Mark off four 1-inch sections on the toilet paper roll. Squeeze the roll flat to cut the pieces.

2. Carefully cut the red felt into strips large enough to cover each napkin ring.

3. Glue a strip of red felt to each piece.

4. Cut heart shapes out of the contrasting color of felt.

5. Glue the hearts onto the napkin ring pieces. Let them dry.

Start by cutting out the rings . . .

Use red felt to cover the rings . . .

Finish your ring by adding some hearts . . .

Your napkin ring adds a festive touch to any Valentine's Day meal!

HOLIDAY HINT:

Use your napkin rings for a Valentine's Day party or give them as a gift.

13

VALENTINE CAT

This valentine cat has a tail with a message.

(use the pattern on page 26, if you like)

WHAT YOU WILL NEED

* red construction paper
* fine-tip marker or pen
* scissors
* white glue
* wiggle eyes
* yarn
* felt (optional)
* glitter (optional)

WHAT TO DO

1. Fold the red construction paper in half to form two rectangles. Draw half a heart (use the pattern on page 26, if you like) and cut it out. This will be the cat's body.

2. Repeat Step 1, making a smaller heart for the cat's head.

3. Position the hearts as shown and glue the pointed ends together. The top heart can overlap the bottom heart.

4. Cut two triangles from the red paper scraps for the cat's ears, or use the patterns on page 28. Glue them on and let them dry.

5. Cut a strip of curved paper for the cat's tail, as shown. Glue it to the cat's back and let it dry.

6. Glue on the wiggle eyes. Let them dry. Then, draw a nose and some stripes with the marker or pen.

7. Glue on some yarn for whiskers. If you like, add some felt for a soft belly and some glitter for the ears.

Glue the hearts together . . .

Start by folding the paper and cutting out a heart . . .

Your cat is ready to celebrate!

Make some ears . . .

15

HOLIDAY HINT:

Write a message on the cat's tail. Then, give this valentine greeting to someone special!

Lacy Valentine Bookmark

Save a place in your favorite book with this bookmark made with lacy valentine hearts.

What You Will Need

- red construction paper
- pencil
- scissors
- white glue
- 3- by 6-inch piece of oak tag or lightweight cardboard
- crayons or markers
- hole punch
- yarn or ribbon

What To Do

1. Draw different heart shapes on the red construction paper. If you like, use the patterns on page 26. Cut out the hearts.

2. Glue the hearts to the oak tag or cardboard. Decorate the bookmark with crayons or markers.

3. Punch a hole in the top of the bookmark.

4. Thread the pieces of yarn or ribbon through the hole. Tie a knot about one inch from the end to form a tassel.

Cut out some hearts to decorate your bookmark . . .

Add some yarn or ribbon . . .

Use the markers for the finishing touches!

LOVE BUG CARD

This love bug hides special messages under its wings. It shows someone how much you care!

WHAT YOU WILL NEED

- ½ sheet red construction paper
- scissors
- ¼ sheet black construction paper
- pen or fine-tip marker
- construction paper in contrasting colors
- wiggle eyes
- white glue
- glitter (optional)
- black pipe cleaner
- clear tape

WHAT TO DO

1. Cut the red construction paper as shown. Fold the corners to make flaps. These will be the bug's wings.

2. Cut a heart shape from the black paper to form the bug's head.

3. Write valentine messages beneath each wing.

4. Cut hearts out of the contrasting colors of paper to decorate the bug's wings.

5. Glue on the hearts and wiggle eyes. Let the glue dry. If you like, add some glitter to make the bug sparkle.

6. Cut the pipe cleaner in half. Tape the two pieces onto the head for antennae.

Start by cutting the paper and folding the corners into wings . . .

I only have eyes for you!

Write a special Valentine's Day message . . .

Cut out hearts and add them to the wings . . .

Add the eyes and antennae . . .

Your love bug is finished!

Heart Ornament

This is a pretty ornament to hang up on Valentine's Day.

What you will need:

- red or pink construction paper
- scissors
- glitter pens, sequins, or stickers
- hole punch
- ribbon or yarn
- white glue

What to do

1. Fold a sheet of paper in half lengthwise.

2. Fold it in half again. Keep folding the paper lengthwise until you have eight sections.

3. Cut heart shapes out of your folded paper. Then, open up the paper and cut it into a large heart, as shown.

4. Decorate the heart with glitter pens, sequins, or stickers.

5. Punch holes in the top of each section, as shown. Loop the ribbon or yarn through the holes and glue the ends to the back. Tape up your ornament.

Start by folding your paper . . .

Cut heart shapes
out of the paper . . .

Cut the folded paper into a heart
and add some ribbon and flowers!

HOLIDAY HINT:

Hang your ornament
where it will remind you
of Valentine's Day!

Valentine Butterfly Paper Clip

This butterfly can be a giant paper clip to give as a Valentine's Day present.

What you will need

* tissue paper
* spring-style clothespin
* construction paper
* scissors
* white glue
* wiggle eyes
* markers or glitter pens
* black pipe cleaner

What to do

1. Fold the tissue paper in half. Fold it half again.

2. Pinch the center of the paper. Insert it into the clothespin.

3. Cut the construction paper into a heart for the butterfly's head. Glue it to the top of the closed end of the clothespin. Let it dry.

4. Glue on the wiggle eyes. Let the glue dry.

5. Use the markers or glitter to make tiny hearts on the butterfly's body.

6. Cut the pipe cleaner in half. Fold the pieces to make antennae. Put a dab of glue in the center of the antennae. Insert them into the clothespin. Let them dry.

Start by folding the tissue paper into a butterfly shape . . .

Cut a heart for the butterfly's head . . .

Add a face and antennae and your butterfly is finished!

Sun Catcher Heart

Hang this sun catcher in the window to see the sun come through.

What You Will Need

- white paper plate
- scissors
- red or pink tissue paper
- wax paper
- white tissue paper
- white glue
- water
- small bowl or paper cup
- paintbrush
- hole punch
- ribbon or yarn
- doily (optional)

What To Do

1. Carefully cut out the center of the paper plate. Then, cut hearts from the red or pink tissue paper.

2. Place the plate on the wax paper face down. Place the white tissue paper over the plate so that the opening is covered.

3. Mix up a thin glue "soup" in the small bowl or paper cup. Use three parts glue to one part water. Stir with the paintbrush, and brush the tissue paper with the glue mixture.

4. Turn the plate over. Glue one heart to the center of the tissue paper. Glue the other hearts to the plate.

5. Leave the plate on the wax paper. Let it dry overnight.

6. When the plate is dry, carefully pull off the wax paper. Punch a hole in the top. Loop the ribbon or yarn through. If you like, you can punch extra holes and loop the ribbon or yarn all the way around, and add a doily for a lacy edge.

Cut out the center of
the paper plate . . .

Mix the water and
glue . . .

Cut some tissue paper . . .

Add the ribbon
and doily for a
nice finish . . .

Hang your beautiful sun
catcher in a window!

HOLIDAY HINT:

Hang this pretty sun catcher
in your window, or give it as
a gift to someone you love.

PATTERNS

Use tracing paper to copy the patterns on these pages. Ask an adult to help you cut and trace the shapes onto construction paper.

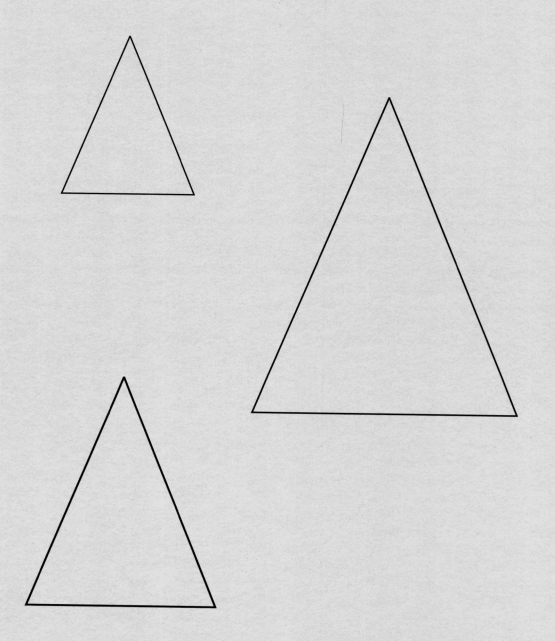

Read About Valentine's Day

Brownrigg, Sheri. *Hearts & Crafts*. Berkeley, Calif.: Tricycle Press, 1996.

Bulla, Clyde Robert. *The Story of Valentine's Day*. New York: HarperCollins Publishers, 1999.

Graham-Barber, Lynda. *Mushy!: The Complete Book of Valentine Words*. New York: Bradbury Press, 1991.

Landau, Elaine. *Valentine's Day—Candy, Love, and Hearts*. Berkeley Heights, N.J.: Enslow Publishers, 2001.

Roop, Peter, and Connie Roop. *Let's Celebrate Valentine's Day*. Brookfield, Conn.: Millbrook Press, 1999.

Ross, Kathy. *All New Crafts for Valentine's Day*. Brookfield, Conn.: Millbrook Press, 2002.

INDEX

A

Amore Napkin
Rings, 12–13

B

Bag of Valentine
Wishes, 6–7
bowl, 8, 24

C

candy, 10
cardboard, 16
clothespin, 22
construction paper,
6, 8, 10, 14, 15, 16,
18, 19, 20, 21, 22
craft sticks, 6
crayons, 6, 16

D

decoupage, 8
doily, 10, 24, 25

F

felt, 12, 13, 14

Fold-up Valentine
Surprise, 10–11
Friendship Necklace,
8–9

G

gift wrap, 8
glitter pens, 6, 14,
18, 20, 22
glue, 6, 8, 10, 11, 12,
14, 15, 16, 18, 20,
22, 24, 25

H

Heart Ornament,
20–21
hole punch, 8, 16,
20, 24
holiday hints, 7, 9,
11, 13, 15, 17, 19,
21, 23, 25

L

Lacy Valentine
Bookmark, 16–17

Love Bug Card,
18–19
Lupercalia, 4

M

magnet, 23
magnetic tape, 23
markers, 6, 14, 16,
17, 18, 22

O

oak tag, 16

P

paintbrush, 8, 24
paint markers, 10
paper bag, 6
paper cup, 8, 24
paper plate, 24, 25
patterns, 26–28
pencils, 8, 10, 12, 16
pens, 14, 18
pipe cleaners, 18, 22
poster board, 8

R

ribbon, 16, 17, 20, 24, 25
Rome, 4–5
ruler, 12

S

scissors, 6, 8, 10, 12, 14, 16,
    18, 20, 22, 24
sequins, 20
stickers, 6, 10, 20
Sun Catcher Heart, 24–25

T

tape, 10, 11, 18
tissue paper, 6, 22, 23, 24, 25
toilet paper roll, 12

toy, 10

V

Valentine Butterfly Paper
    Clip, 22–23
Valentine Cat, 14–15
Valentine's Day, 4–5

W

water, 8, 24, 25
wax paper, 8, 24
wiggle eyes, 14, 18, 19, 22

Y

yarn, 8, 14, 16, 17, 20, 24